Paint With Words

Fresh Language For Irresistible Writing

Graeme Dinnen

Contents

13. Book Recommendations   74

Chapter One

The Starting Line

Great writers don't just hand you a new angle on life; they shove it in your face and dare you to own it. They make you see the world in their particular, messy, brilliant way. In the process, they teach you the art of having a voice that isn't timid, polite, or apologetic. They teach you to roar in your own accent.

Welcome, then, to this curious, ink-smudged funfair we call writing.

If you're here to pen books, articles, newsletters, blogs, or merely to stop your webpages from looking like the digital equivalent of a beige waiting room, you've set off on a splendid and exasperating expedition.

Writing is equal parts alchemy and archaeology: you're digging for treasure and melting it down at the same time.

Think of your writing as a compass, if only one bought from a slightly suspect stall in a foreign market. It's here to help you sketch scenes that cling to your reader like perfume on a silk scarf.

Type a query into your search bar asking how to write a book and it will dutifully disgorge a checklist of the obvious: know your audience, polish your "author brand," be clear, be concise, mind your grammar, keep the pace jaunty but not breathless, ensure a pleasing narrative arc, check your facts, don't plagiarise, and so forth.

It's the literary equivalent of being told to floss and eat your greens.

If you've seen the 1989 film Dead Poets Society, you'll remember that glorious moment when John Keating (Robin Williams with his soul bared) invites his students to rip out the pompous preface by author Dr. J. Evans Pritchard. It's one of cinema's great acts of academic vandalism. Keating isn't being anarchic for fun; he's making the point that poetry, and by extension all art, is strangled by the calipers and tick-boxes of formula.

You cannot quantify a heartbeat.

Yes, the standard checklist of advice has its place. It can even be useful, in the way that stabilisers are useful when you're small and wobbly. But there will always be room for the writer who tears up the blueprint, rebels against conformity and listens instead to the unruly, disobedient thump of their own voice.

The Opening Sentence

The opening sentence of a book, an article or anything written for others to read, is the billet-doux and the battering ram, the soft handshake and the unapologetic slap. It's the moment a writer either seduces you into the room or leaves you lingering awkwardly on the threshold, wondering if you shouldn't have stayed home.

All the rest, every elegant pirouette of prose, every clever aside, is hostage to that opening line's success. It must promise without boasting, tease without grovelling, and carry, in its small suitcase, the whole swaggering intention of what follows.

Get it right, and the reader will trust you; get it wrong, and they'll wander off to make tea, forgetting entirely why they came.

Some examples of memorable opening sentences in books:

- **"Call me Ishmael."** *Herman Melville, Moby-Dick* (1851). It's not stating a fact, it's more of a command. The narrator is introducing himself to you in a way that makes you feel he is an assertive person, and about what you are getting yourself into with the coming story.

- **"It was the best of times, it was the worst of times....."** *Charles Dickens, A Tale of Two Cities* (1859)

- **"All happy families are alike; each unhappy family is unhappy in its own way."** *Leo Tolstoy, Anna Karenina* (1878)

- **"It is a truth universally acknowledged, that a single man in possession of a good fortune, must be in want of a wife."** *Jane Austen, Pride and Prejudice*

- **"We were somewhere around Barstow on the edge of the desert when the drugs began to take hold,"** Fear and Loathing in Las Vegas, Hunter S. Thompson (1971)

We humans remember only a sliver of what we hear and a scrap of what we see, but vivid images? Those imprint themselves into our minds. So make your opening lines vivid enough to be remembered.

Now let us embrace metaphors and similes, those show ponies of prose, trotted out to do the heavy lifting of imagination.

Metaphors are the shortcut, the express lift to the penthouse of meaning; similes are their chatty cousins, forever comparing one thing to another because silence makes them nervous.

Both are the difference between writing that merely informs and writing that seduces.

Forget the paralysing dread of the blank page, that silent reproach to your intellect. This is your rescue boat, tossed into the doldrums of dreary prose like a flare.

Ever wondered how to describe a sunset without leaning on the same clichés used by romantics and real estate agents? Here's your armoury, bright, polished, and occasionally dangerous.

We'll rummage around inside the machinery of writing, poking fingers into the cogs to understand why a good sentence sings and a bad one sulks in the corner.

Whatever you're writing, the same framework applies. Writing isn't just communication; it's teleportation. With nothing more than your breath and a keyboard, you can whisk readers from one century to another, from a tepid suburb to the lip of a volcano.

Words bend time. They are your wand, your weapon, your passport.

Chapter Two

Threads That Hold Prose Together

Metaphors

Metaphors are not decorations. They're oxygen. They give the reader lungs to breathe the world you're building. They take the abstract, the slippery, the invisible, and turn it into something you can actually stub your toe on.

A well-loaded metaphor can carry an entire chapter on its back. Try extended ones; let them unfurl across paragraphs like a banner in a stiff wind.

Surprise yourself, and you'll surprise everyone else.

Similes

Similes, meanwhile, are the training wheels of imagination, "like" and "as" keeping everyone steady. When done well, they can be tiny fireworks in your prose: brief, bright, delightful.

When done badly, they appeal with the grace of a shopping cart with one bad wheel.

Play with rhythm. Let a simile slip in like a whispered aside, or crash down like a cymbal. Unexpectedness is the charm: compare a lying politician to Pinocchio's extending nose, a memory to a moth circling a bare bulb.

Make associations that make the reader mutter, *"Oh, that's rather good,"* before they realise they've been seduced.

Useful Phrases

Useful phrases are the spice rack of writing. A pinch too little and everything tastes like boiled cabbage; too much and you've committed a literary mugging.

Adjectives, adverbs, action verbs and idioms. Deploy them with the calculated care of a maître d' adding truffle shavings. You want flavour, not flatulence.

Headlines

Headlines are the pick-up lines of prose. If they don't provoke a second glance, the evening is over before it's begun. Give your headlines some swagger. Some promise. A wink, even. Wordplay, alliteration, a whiff of danger. Whatever it takes to lure your reader inside.

Quotes

A well-chosen quote is like seating an eloquent guest at your table who graciously does some of the talking for you. Choose wisely, though. Too many, and it looks as if you've invited people over only to abandon them with strangers.

Attention-Resetting Techniques

Readers, bless them, have the attention span of caffeinated ferrets. You'll need cliffhangers, flashbacks, foreshadowing; anything that nudges, jolts, or sweet-talks them into turning the page.

Suspense isn't an accident; it's carpentry.

Transitions

Transitions are the quiet servants of writing. Invisible when they do their job well; catastrophically noticeable when they don't. They keep the reader gliding instead of stopping to re-read the sentence. Add them with a light hand. Think velvet rope, not barbed wire.

Writing is not about praise, prizes, or bestseller lists lined with novels about lonely detectives and traumatised heiresses. It's about connection, about reaching out through the fog and tapping someone on the shoulder with nothing but ink and intention.

Learn your audience: their cravings, their fears, their late-night worries. Take risks, write boldly, and don't shuffle along in the safe rut that's already filled with thousands of timid sentences. Attend workshops, argue with editors, read until your eyes blur.

And then write again.

Because writing is a long, absurd, wonderful pilgrimage. And if you do it well, if you do it honestly, you might just leave a fingerprint on someone's soul.

Now go on. The page is waiting.

And, like you, it hates to be kept waiting.

Chapter Three

The Power of Metaphors and Similes

Metaphors and similes are the salt and saffron of prose, those extravagant seasonings that turn a plain linguistic stew into something worth lingering over.

They are the linguistic illusionists of literature, pulling rabbits, doves, and occasionally entire emotional histories out of the hat of an otherwise innocent sentence.

Used properly, they take the pedestrian and elevate it, sometimes all the way to the penthouse suite of meaning.

Metaphors, the more enigmatic and slippery of the pair, operate like secret doors in an old hotel. Push the right panel, and it leads you to a different room entirely, usually one you didn't know existed.

People "get" metaphors. Our brains are wired for images – metaphors are images in words – metaphors paint pictures in readers minds. They carry emotional associations that resonate instantly with readers and stitch together ideas that shouldn't logically belong to one another, but somehow do in that moment of revelation. A writer who understands metaphors is a jeweller of thought, cutting, shaping, polishing.

Take Sylvia Plath in **The Bell Jar,** likening life to a fig tree, each fruit a bright, bulging possibility until the whole bounty rots while you dither. Or Steve Jobs, enticing John Sculley to leave Pepsi and join Apple as CEO, "Do you want to make sugared water for the rest of your life, or do you want a chance to transform the world?"

It's a metaphor that does more than illuminate; it indicts. It presses a finger on your chest and asks, Well? Are you choosing, or are you waiting, too?

Similes, meanwhile, are the magpies of literary devices, flashy, charming, endlessly attracted to glitter. They hang their comparisons from the branches of sentences like bits of tinsel, catching the reader's eye with a quick glint.

Two little words, like or as, and suddenly the page is breathing in colour and texture. Fitzgerald knew how to wield them with enviable nonchalance.

"The lights grew brighter as the earth lurched away from the sun." (The Great Gatsby)

Fitzgerald uses planetary movement to convey the rising energy of Gatsby's parties. The simile exaggerates the setting, making the night feel cosmically charged, as though the party controls the world's rotation.

"Her voice was like smoke, soft, curling, elusive." (The God of Small Things)
Arundhati Roy compares a voice to smoke conveying something intimate yet untouchable, a presence that fills the air without ever being held.

Yet these devices do far more than decorate. They are emotional detonators, small charges placed under the floorboards of the reader's sensibility.

A well-cast metaphor can gut you with a single image. Emily Dickinson's *"Hope is the thing with feathers"* is a perfect example, conveying a sense of fragile, persistent optimism that flutters just out of reach but never quite flies away.

Yet, and this is a very large yet, there is a danger here. A writer drunk on metaphors is as unbearable as a man who wears too much cologne: over-whelming, cloying, and ultimately repellent.

The art lies in choosing the right comparisons, the way a good chef selects ingredients; not every-thing goes with everything, and too much of a good thing is still too much.

When used with a little judgement and a dash of daring, metaphors and similes can turn prose into something symphonic - language that resonates, that lingers, that offers readers not merely a story but an experience.

They are the quiet magicians of writing, trans-forming words into something larger than them-selves, leaving the reader somewhere new, some-where truer than where they began.

Chapter Four

Crafting Engaging Metaphors

To unleash the power of linguistic alchemy, metaphors are the conjuring trick of language, turning the flat grey of life into something worth licking the spoon for. From another perspective, they are interventions dressed up as parables.

They're the writer's philosopher's stone, capable of transforming a misshapen sentence into a shimmering insight.

So, if we're going to talk about crafting them, let's do it properly, because a good metaphor is never an accident, and a bad one is never forgotten.

1. Embracing the Subtle Nuances

Every word is a tiny wardrobe leading to an undiscovered Narnia with layers of meaning, etymological detritus and cultural baggage, all waiting to ambush the inattentive.

When you build a metaphor, you dig, not politely with a trowel, but with the enthusiasm of a dog burying a stolen bone. Unearth the historical echoes, the side-eye connotations, the smirking ambiguities.

Choose the words that hum with the exact frequency of what you want to say. Do this, and your metaphors won't just sit there, they'll glow.

2. The Enigmatic Charm of Extended Metaphors

Extended metaphors are the slow-cooked stew of the literary kitchen. Anyone can fling in a quick comparison, but to nurture a metaphor through paragraphs is to build a world with its own weather.

Set it up at the start, then let it hum in the background, resurfacing throughout the plot like a well-funded opera's favourite refrain.

Done right, it pulls the reader along in a web of associations that feels inevitable in hindsight, though you and I know it's anything but.

3. Balancing Familiarity and Innovation

Metaphors thrive at that delicious little crossroads where the familiar bumps into the unexpected and spills its drink. You want readers to recognise the feeling but blink at the phrasing.

Avoid clichés. They're metaphors that died in committee. Instead, prod the edges of the ordinary. Make fresh connections without abandoning sense altogether.

The trick is surprise, not bewilderment.

4. Illuminating the Abstract

Abstract ideas float around like balloons filled with philosophical hot air. A metaphor gives them ballast. Emotion, time, the whole shimmering mess of human consciousness. These are slippery customers.

A good metaphor pins ideas down long enough for the reader to examine them, like a butterfly briefly consenting to land on a fingertip. Translate the ineffable into something you could drop on your foot.

5. Engaging the Senses

Most metaphors aim at the eyes, which is a pity because the rest of the senses feel left out and sulk. Why not give them something to do?

Smuggle in scents, textures, the aftertaste of something bitter or sweet. A metaphor that touches all the senses becomes not a picture but an experience, more immersive than any VR headset and significantly less ridiculous-looking.

6. The Unbridled Play of Creativity

Metaphors are where the writer gets to misbehave. Let the imagination off the leash. Juxtapose the improbable with the perfectly obvious. Make connections that astonish even you. There's joy in metaphor-making, a sort of linguistic treasure-hunting where the reward is the sudden glint of a phrase that feels both impossible and inevitable.

The more you explore, the richer the trove becomes.

To craft metaphors, cultivate the gaze of someone who notices everything from the crack in the pavement, the eyebrow twitch, or the way steam coils in the same upward spiral of a ghost emerging from a kettle.

Inspiration is everywhere; the art lies in recognising it and buffing it until it sparkles. With each metaphor, you're not merely decorating your prose; you're inviting readers into a place where language grows larger than itself. Where truths sneak out from behind the words and tug at sleeves.

Some examples to conjure images;

"It's the choice between dysentery and diarrhoea."

"And like dog years, airport minutes should be multiplied by seven."

"He's barking up the wrong tree, and he's not even in the right forest."

"He moved with the speed of a man twice his size."

"There are more holes in that argument than on a golf course."

William Shakespeare engaged his audience with well-placed metaphors:

"Juliet is the sun" (Romeo and Juliet)

"Life's but a walking shadow" (Macbeth)

"All the world's a stage" (As You Like It)

"Denmark is a prison" (Hamlet)

""Cry 'Havoc!' and let slip the dogs of war." (Julius Caesar)

"We are such stuff as dreams are made on" (The Tempest)

When Apple's Steve Jobs was enticing John Sculley, Marketing Executive at Pepsi to join Apple, he used a now-famous metaphor as a convincer: ***"Do you want to make sugared water for the rest of your life, or do you want a chance to transform the world?"***

Chapter Five

Creating Vivid Similes

Similes are the little black dress of writing: deceptively simple, flattering on everyone, and entirely capable of stealing the show if accessorised with a bit of nerve.

They're the comparisons we make when we want language to stop slouching and start vogueing.

A good simile doesn't just illuminate. It struts in, grabs the whole sentence by the lapels, and says, "Right, listen to this."

Let's explore the tricky art of crafting similes that sparkle, not the ones that feel like a weak handshake.

1. Pensive Subject Selection (Or Stop Comparing Everything to the Moon)

If you want a simile that sticks, choose subjects with personality. It's the literary equivalent of inviting your whacky aunt to dinner instead of your dull cousin who collects train timetables.

Pick things with texture, strangeness, contradictions. Give your reader a comparison that tickles the imagination rather than patting it politely on the head.

The aim is not to explain, but to seduce the reader into seeing your point as if it were their own idea.

2. Evoking Sensory Splendour

A simile should hit the senses like a brass band. Too many writers fire off similes that only appeal to the eyes - visual but lifeless, like a bowl of wax fruit.

Be greedy. Wake every sense. Tempt them. Tease them.

Instead of: *"The smell of coffee drifted through the room"*, try something a little more operatic: *"The coffee aroma rose like a baritone serenade, earthy, smug and determined to rouse every half-dead soul within sniffing radius."*

Now that's a simile that earns its keep.

3. An Intricate Balancing Act

Similes shine because they can show contrast or similarity with a flick of the wrist. Want to show strength?

Try: *"Her resilience was as unyielding as an oak, rooted deeply in stubbornness and entirely unamused by passing storms."*

It's equal parts insight and insult, which is exactly where good writing lives.

4. Skirting the Fringes of Cliché

Clichés are the instant coffee of comparisons - quick, easy, and thoroughly disappointing. Nothing sends a reader packing faster than a simile that's been reheated since the 18th century.

Avoid *"clear as crystal," "busy as a bee,"* and anything that sounds like it should be cross-stitched onto a cushion.

Instead, go rogue: *"Clarity as sharp as a diamond's facet, slicing a neat path through the fog of confusion."*

Anne Miller's wise warning: *"A cliché a day keeps the reader away."*

Examples to avoid like undercooked chicken: Think outside the box – Grab the bull by the horns – It goes without saying – Every cloud has a silver lining – There's no 'I' in team – At the end of the day (unless you actually mean the end of a day)

5. The Esoteric World of Style and Word-play

Similes are marvellous places to be a bit of a show-off. They let you twist grammar, shift rhythm, and create little linguistic firework displays, provided you don't burn your eyebrows in the process.

Think of them as the percussion section of your prose. They should add texture, snap, and the occasional cymbal crash, not drown out the orchestra.

6. Ascending the Tower of Revision

Revision is where similes go to grow up or die heroically. The first draft often produces similes that sound as though they were written by an exhausted schoolteacher.

Read them aloud. Do they sound brilliant? Keep them. Do they sound like a greeting card? Bin them.

Give them to a friend. If they squint or look pained, revise. If they laugh, keep it. If they snort tea out their nose, frame it.

By mastering vivid similes, you unlock the glorious ability to make your writing fizz, crackle and misbehave in all the right ways.

The goal is not just to compare, but to enchant, to give readers a literary cocktail loaded with imagery, wit, and just a hint of danger.

Examples (Delightfully Ridiculous and Surprisingly Useful)

• He rose from the chair like a balloon trying not to look obvious about floating away.• It's what's inside that matters, just like a fridge.• It stuck out like a unicycle at a Hells Angels' rally. • It's as practical as using a string vest to carry water. • It sucks when the market jacks you around like that hot girl (or guy) from school who knew exactly what they were doing.

William Shakespeare's contribution includes:

"My love is as deep as the sea." (Romeo and Juliet)

"Look like the innocent flower, but be the serpent under't." (Macbeth)

"I am constant as the northern star." (Julius Caesar)

"The moon, like to a silver bow." (A Midsummer Night's Dream)

"True as steel." (As You Like It)

Chapter Six

The Value of Useful Phrases

Writing, at its best, is a kind of sorcery. The right phrase, placed with the precision of a jeweller setting a stone, can lift a paragraph from the merely competent into something that tingles the skin.

A well-chosen string of words can cartwheel readers into new landscapes, stir sentiments they didn't know they possessed, and leave an aftertaste that lingers long after the page is turned.

If you're serious about writing anything worth remembering, learning to wield useful phrases is not optional; it's essential kit.

But before you festoon your prose with ornamentation, understand this: a phrase isn't useful because it's pretty. It earns its keep. It clarifies, heightens, deepens.

It shows the reader something they didn't know they'd noticed. Useful phrases come in many guises - metaphors that detonate meaning, similes that glide in under the radar, imagery that grabs you by the lapels and insists on being felt.

This craft demands taste and discrimination. Each phrase must justify the space it occupies.

Ask yourself: Why is this here? Is it sharpening what's fuzzy, anchoring what's slippery, or coaxing forth the precise emotion you're after?

If the answer is *"it just sounded nice,"* that's your cue to swing the axe.

Tone, too, is a stern taskmaster. Your voice determines the phrases you're allowed to get away with. In a conversational piece, you can scatter around little whimsies, words that skip, phrases that wink.

"Dancing on air," "a burst of laughter" - they're the confetti of language, and there's nothing wrong with a little confetti in the right room. In more sober writing, however, such flourishes stick out like a flamingo at a funeral.

Choose accordingly.

Clichés will beckon. Ignore them. They are linguistic leftovers: convenient, easy, and invariably stale. To truly enchant a reader, you need phrases that feel as though they were discovered, not inherited.

That requires rummaging around in unfamiliar corners of thought, mixing odd ingredients, and reaching past the obvious into the untried.

And then there's rhythm, the secret scaffolding of good writing. A phrase can be exquisite in isolation but disastrous in context if it trips the reader or snags the tempo.

Your prose should move with the grace of a well-rehearsed dancer, and your phrases should slip into that choreography, not stomp all over it.

Where does one find such phrases? By paying attention to everything. The world is an overflowing pantry of sensory detail: colours that bruise the sky, the unnerving rattle of a snake's presence, the melancholy smell of old paper.

Watch people: *"I like to watch people. Sometimes I ride the subway all day and look at them and listen to them. I just want to figure out who they are and what they want and where they're going."* Ray Bradbury.

Watch cities: *"If you are lucky enough to have lived in Paris as a young man, then wherever you* *go for the rest of your life, it stays with you, for Paris is a moveable feast. "* Ernest Hemingway.

Watch weather: *"But who wants to be foretold the weather? It is bad enough when it comes, without our having the misery of knowing about it before-hand."* Jerome K. Jerome.

Writers are hoarders of moments; useful phrases are forged from the scraps we collect.

Films are a treasure trove, too. Screenwriters are paid to bottle dialogue that sounds true, even when it isn't.

I've been fortunate enough to glean wisdom from friends who stitch together such lines for a living: Ray Singer and Eugenia Bostwick-Singer who wrote the screenplay for Mulan, and Peter Bellwood, screenwriter for the film Highlander.

They taught me that a great phrase is never stolen whole: it's kneaded, stretched, interpreted.

Inspiration is fair game; plagiarism is not. Credit what you borrow, and respect what isn't yours. Above all, read. Read like a starving person at a banquet. Read the classics, the contemporary, the weird, the forgotten. The more voices you absorb, the more agile your own becomes.

A wide palate of language makes it easier to craft phrases that feel alive rather than assembled.

A good friend takes reading to absurd lengths. On one occasion he went to the kitchen to get cutlery. Several minutes later, I found him absorbed in the newspaper he'd used to line the cutlery drawer.

Moderation is key. Tattoo that into your brain. Stuff your writing with too many fancy turns of phrase and you don't impress the reader, you bludgeon them. • Writers should eschew sesquipedalian obfuscation because prolix verbosity paradoxically undermines communicative clarity.

Useful phrases should be the bright strokes on the canvas, not the whole painting. Let each one matter.

In the end, the art of the useful phrase is what separates the pedestrian from the memorable. Choose with intention. Write with rhythm. Notice the world. Feed your vocabulary.

And then, with a little alchemy, turn those raw materials into lines that breathe.

Examples of evocative phrases
• The cemetery of dreams and ideas you've given up on
• He's not an alcoholic; he just drinks like an Irishman
• Along with everything else, right now, crystal balls are in short supply
• Pay attention. This has value for everyone in possession of a heartbeat.

• The sidewalks are broken and disorderly; we stumble down the streets as if we have a drinking problem

• An anthem for those who still dream about little moments in life

Chapter Seven

Captivating Headlines and Sub-Headlines

How to Stop Your Writing Dressing in Beige and Start Making It Strut

Headlines are the sequinned jackets of writing. They walk into the room five minutes before you do, wink suggestively at the reader, and dare them not to look.

Sub-headlines are their slightly more sensible siblings: still glamorous, but wearing shoes you can actually walk in. Together, they are the make-or-break double act of your prose.

Without them, even the most dazzling piece of writing lies abandoned like a gourmet meal left on a night bus.

If your headline doesn't grab them by the collar and growl *"You need this,"* they're gone, off to look at pictures of sourdough.

The Purpose of Headlines (Other Than Saving Your Work from Anonymity)

A good headline is not a title. It's a promise, made with the swagger of someone who fully intends to keep it.

It should:
• arrest attention,
• whisper seductively about what's inside, and
• imply that failing to click is a moral failing.
A headline is the literary equivalent of shouting *"Free booze!"* across a crowded bar room.
A sub-headline is the polite follow-up that explains what kind and when.

Crafting Headlines That Grab, Grapple and Won't Let Go

Use words that punch, shimmy, or at the very least, poke the reader firmly in the ribs.

Think about the feeling you want to spark. Suspense? Awe? Mild existential panic?

Instead of limp, apologetic offerings like: *"A Crime Story"*, try something that sounds like it smokes cigars and has opinions: *"A Twisted Tale of Deception and Danger That Will Leave You Breathless"*

It's not subtle. Subtlety is for gardeners and Swiss watchmakers.

Headlines must swagger. Be Specific, or Be Ignored

Vague headlines are the literary version of hospital food: unidentifiable, unloved, and swiftly avoided.

Highlight what's unique about your piece. What makes it yours and not the identical article three pixels below it?

A headline should shine like a mad Victorian explorer promising you wonders you can't pronounce: *"An Unforgettable Adventure Through Time and Space"*

It says, *"Click me. I'm interesting. I'm not like the others."*

Sub-Headlines: The Supporting Cast Who Deserve Their Own Trailer

Think of sub-headlines as the charming maître d' who guides readers through the restaurant of your argument without losing their reservation or their patience.

They.....

• break the text into digestible delights,
• set expectations, and
• keep the reader from wandering off in search of snacks.

Keep them short, sharp, and helpful, like a good tailor.

Experiment. Yes. Even the weird ideas

Try wordplay, alliteration, questions, or something slightly cheeky.Readers enjoy being teased. They enjoy being challenged. They enjoy, above all, not being bored.

Just keep your tone consistent. If your headline is doing high kicks, your sub-headline cannot sit down quietly and knit socks.

In Short: Headlines Are the Peacock Feathers of Your Writing

They must seduce, intrigue, and smuggle readers into the main event before they can change their minds.

Use powerful language, avoid the beige fog of vagueness, and tinker until it all shines.

Your headline is the first handshake with your reader and the one that decides whether they stay long enough to hear the joke.

Examples
• Friend or Faux?
• A Black Belt in Bad Decisions
• Sweet and Saudi
• Life Without Barriers
• Pause and Effect

Chapter Eight

Adding Impact with Useful Quotes

Quotes are peculiar little things. They arrive pre-polished, wisdom with the bark taken off, and yet they continue to chime across centuries, connecting strangers with the ease of gossip and the gravitas of scripture.

For a writer, wielding a good quote is like slipping a hand into an old, well-made glove: it lets you touch the world with a little more finesse.

Used properly, quotes lend your prose a timbre that lingers after the page is turned.

Let's wander, without hurry, through the art of using them well.

1. Mine the Literary Lodes

The canon is embarrassingly rich. Shakespeare muttering delicious truths about love and ambition; Plato and Nietzsche poking at the soft underbelly of morality and existence. These lines have survived precisely because they are better than most of what we'll manage ourselves.

But pluck with care. A misapplied quote is the writer's version of wearing evening shoes to the beach: technically allowed, but everyone will notice the mismatch.

Understand what the quote says, what it meant when it was written, and why you're borrowing it now. Otherwise, it just clutters the room.

2. Add Your Own Scars and Stories

Famous voices carry authority, but your own voice carries intimacy. A personal anecdote, small and unassuming, can illuminate a paragraph like a match in a dark hallway.

When braided with the words of others, your experiences give the piece a heartbeat.

Just don't turn your essay into a memoir unless that's the point. Let your stories serve the quote, not smother it.

3. Use Culture and History with Respect

A well-placed historical quote drops your reader into an era with cinematic neatness. Mandela on perseverance, Gandhi on conscience, All carry the freight of struggle and triumph.

But context matters. Misunderstand a reference, and the effect is less profound and more pratfall.

Between songs, Robbie Williams once playfully belted out *"Deutschland über alles"* to a Nuremberg crowd, blissfully unaware of the historical baggage. Eighty thousand Germans booed. Always check the provenance before you parade the past.

4. Amplify the Quieter Voices

The world isn't short of clever things said by the usual suspects, but sometimes wisdom comes from the overlooked, the unquoted, the unglamorous, the unfashionable.

Giving these voices room on your page not only expands your reader's horizon but cultivates a more generous kind of storytelling.

And please: attribute properly. Misquoting is the literary equivalent of handing back the wrong coat at the cloakroom.

Consider the misquote *"money is the root of all evil"* that should read *"For the love of money is the root of all evil."* Or the endlessly fabricated *"Beam me up, Scotty"*, words that were never actually spoken. It was *"Scotty, beam me up."* Same words, different sequence.

Check your sources unless you enjoy being corrected by someone unbearably pleased with themselves.

5. Practise the Art of Being Brief

The power of a quote often lies in its compression. It distils, no fat, no filler. Try doing the same. A line of prose trimmed to its essence can hit with the same arresting clarity.

However, economy is not the same as opacity. Be sparing, not cryptic.

6. Scavenge Beyond Books

Wisdom abounds in films, songs, graffiti, even the occasional lucid social-media post. Popular culture leaves a breadcrumb trail of quotable lines that readers recognise immediately.

These snippets can animate your writing, giving it texture and tempo.

In the end, using quotes is a balancing act. Your voice, their voices, all in conversation. None shouting, none whispering.

When you get it right, your writing feels both broader and deeper, as though it's standing on the shoulders of a crowd.

Examples to Keep in Your Back Pocket
Not bespoke to your subject, but useful ammunition nonetheless. Note, mercifully, no *"food for thought"* clichés here:

"On your last day on earth, the person you became will meet the person you could have become." Anonymous

"Wise men speak because they have something to say; fools because they have to say something." Plato

"A compromise is an agreement between two men to do what both agree is wrong." Lord Edward Cecil

"That men do not learn very much from the lessons of history is the most important of all the lessons of history." Aldous Huxley

"I always wanted to be somebody. Now I realise I should have been more specific." Lily Tomlin

"Be kind, for everyone you meet is fighting a battle you know nothing about." Attributed to Ian Maclaren

Chapter Nine

Attention-Resetting Techniques

In the whirling centrifuge of modern life, where attention is shorter than a fruit fly's lifespan, holding a reader's focus is less a craft and more a contact sport.

Every writer must learn the art of the nudge, the subtle recalibration of attention, before the reader wanders off to scroll something shiny.

Think of these techniques as gentle slaps to the narrative's cheeks, little reminders that something worth staying for is happening on the page.

They are not tricks; tricks are for magicians and politicians. These are structural recalibrations, shifts in tempo, tone, or intrigue that tug the reader back by the collar just as they're about to drift into the ennui of distraction.

And here's a truth seldom mentioned but always felt: writing isn't finished when you reach the end. It's finished when you've come back, wincing at your own excesses, and pared the thing down to its fighting weight.

Revision is the writer's version of honesty - painful, necessary, revealing. Read your work, or have it read aloud. Listen for the moments that sag. Tighten them. Reinforce them. Replace them. Attention, after all, is a precious resource; don't squander it.

Effective attention-resetting comes dressed in many forms:

• A cliffhanger slinking in at the end of a paragraph.• A character who refuses to behave.• Dialogue sharp enough to draw blood. • White space that breathes like a yoga instructor. • A twist you didn't see coming but now can't imagine the piece without. • A visual that arrests the mind like a stop sign in a blizzard. • A personal anecdote slipped in like a conspiratorial wink.

These devices don't simply decorate your prose. They aerate it. They keep the reader awake, alert, alive to possibility. They remind your audience why they're still here and why leaving would be a regrettable decision.

Return often to your draft. Prod it. Question it. Ask yourself the most important question of all: Is this interesting? If the answer is anything less than an enthusiastic yes, sharpen your knives and edit again.

Incorporate these techniques with style and a little swagger, and your writing won't just hold attention; it will command it, the way a good sermon commands the congregation.

Readers will follow you willingly, eagerly, hungrily, right to the last line, and then ask for seconds.

Examples of attention-resetting questions

Why do I write this?

Still not convinced?

Does this sound like you?

What makes this so special?

Think I'm exaggerating?

See the difference?

Maintaining Momentum and Flow

If you want to keep your readers not merely awake but willingly captive, you must learn the delicate, almost balletic art of momentum.

Nothing kills a piece of writing faster than a patch of prose that flops onto the page like a damp sock.

Confusion, stagnation, meandering digressions, these are the vandals of narrative flow. Your job is to keep them out, preferably with a very large stick.

Momentum in writing isn't speed; it's direction. It's the sense that each sentence leans ever so slightly into the next, like dominoes with ambition.

This is where transitions come in, those modest little ushers of language: "however," "therefore," "moreover", words that don't draw attention to themselves but quietly make sure everyone knows where to go next.

Use them with intention, as if you were guiding readers through a gallery where one wrong turn lands them in the storeroom instead of the exhibition.

The aim is a narrative that never jolts, never lurches, never throws the reader out of the moving vehicle.

You want glide. You want drift. You want that seamless sensation of being carried along by a current you barely notice until you're waist-deep.

Cohesion, too, is part of the architecture. Pronouns that point back like polite hosts. Repetition that underscores without browbeating. Parallel structures that give your prose the pleasing symmetry of a well-laid table.

These devices act as tiny handrails, allowing the reader to navigate your thoughts without slipping on the tiles of complexity.

Do this well and your writing becomes a guided tour rather than a treasure hunt. No reader will be left blinking in the wrong corridor, wondering how they got there or why.

Chapter Ten

Smooth Transitions

One of the silent killers of a reader's attention is the clunky transition.

Nothing jolts someone out of a story faster than a paragraph that doesn't know where it's going, or a chapter that arrives like an uninvited guest.

Smooth transitions are the unsung heroes of writing. They're the oil that keeps the gears turning, the red carpet that guides readers from one idea to the next without them noticing the direction.

Seamless transitions require more than glueing sentences together. You must understand the trajectory of your narrative, the rise and fall of tension, and the connections between ideas.

Each shift, between sentences, paragraphs, or chapters, should feel inevitable, like a conversation you can't help but follow. The reader should never have to stop and wonder, How did we get here?

Certain words act as understated signposts: "however," "so," "beyond that," "on the other hand." They whisper, Pay attention; something is changing, and they prepare the reader for the next beat.

Think of them as bridges over a river: without them, readers might plunge into confusion; with them, they cross effortlessly, eyes still on the scenery, not the footing.

Beyond single sentences, a summary or linking paragraph at the end of a section can serve as connective tissue. By recapping key points and highlighting the central theme, you give the reader both context and anticipation, like that maître d', reminding you that your next course will be exquisite.

Referencing earlier ideas is another trick in your toolkit. A well-placed looping callback or thematic echo reinforces cohesion, emphasises significance and deepens the reader's understanding.

Interwoven themes create a narrative fabric that's impossible to tear at a casual glance; readers become immersed in the web you've spun, following threads they didn't even know were leading them.

Pacing is everything. Abrupt transitions slam readers out of the story; overly long ones lull them into disengagement. The art lies in balance: enough to signal a shift, but subtle enough that the flow feels effortless.

Mastering transitions isn't just a matter of craft. It's a gateway to narrative control. With each carefully designed bridge, you lead readers from one idea to the next with grace and authority, leaving them engrossed, eager, and fully immersed in the unfolding story.

Examples of momentum-keeping transitions

By contrast...
To top it off...
Beyond that...
Or even better...
But that's not all...
The answer might surprise you.
The trick is to...

The simple truth is: flow is not accidental. It is engineered, finessed, and maintained with the care of someone who knows exactly where they're taking their reader, and intends to deliver them there in style.

With transitions handled deftly, your writing achieves that rare state where readers move from paragraph to paragraph, chapter to chapter, almost without thinking, and yet, at the end, they look back and realise they've been carried effortlessly through something both intelligent and enjoyable.

More Writing Tips

Coming across dense paragraphs is like running into a brick wall made of words. The kind that makes a reader reach for a bookmark, muttering curses under their breath, because they know they'll need a good night's sleep, perhaps a lie-in, to rebuild reserves of mental energy required to carry on.

The authors whose sentences stretch like elastic, include William Faulkner, that Southern conjurer of endless passages especially in Absalom, Absalom! and The Sound and the Fury, where paragraphs sprawl like lazy rivers, carrying consciousness and time in their muddied currents.

But if you're chasing the crown for sheer endurance, look no further than Joyce's Ulysses: Molly Bloom's monologue barrels on for over 4,000 words without a single full stop, a literary marathon that makes your average novel look like a hastily scribbled shopping list.

Chapter Eleven

Summary

1 Read like a writer

It's difficult to write well if you don't read widely. Pay attention to how others construct sentences, build tension, and use rhythm. Read both inside and outside your comfort zone.

2. Show, don't tell

Don't just say someone is angry, describe the trembling hands, the tight jaw, the sharp words. Make readers feel it.

3. Write with clarity

Clear writing beats clever writing almost every time. Avoid unnecessary jargon, convoluted sentences, or filler words that slow the reader down.

4. Find your voice

Your unique voice is your fingerprint on the page. Experiment, take risks, and let your personality come through.

5. Rewrite mercilessly

Your first draft is never perfect. Trim excess, sharpen verbs, and cut the clichés. Good writing is largely about rewriting.

6. Pay attention to rhythm

Sentence length, paragraph breaks, and punctuation all affect flow. Read aloud to hear the music of your prose. If you're intent on winding the tension tight, take a leaf from Agatha Christie, who pared her sentences down to the bone as her readers turned the last few pages

7. Keep a notebook

Ideas strike at odd moments. Capture them - phrases, observations, sparks of dialogue - so they can grow into something larger later.

8. Avoid "writerly" habits

Adverbs and passive voice often weaken prose. Trust strong nouns and verbs to carry your meaning.

9. Write when you feel like it

Writing 200 words a day keeps your writing muscles active but if you feel like writing once a fortnight, setting your alarm for 4am or creating a book slowly over 5 years, do it. Sometimes a discipline is what you need to get the momentum started. You can still succeed even if you break many of the so-called "writing rules".

10. Know your reader, but don't pander

Write with someone in mind, but don't sacrifice authenticity for approval. Great writing challenges readers as much as it entertains them.

11. Ask Yourself "Why should they care"?

People only give attention to things that are relevant to them. We are goal-seeking beings and so before extolling the virtues of your book, blog or article, focus on the person you're trying to communicate with, what simply calls out to use that'll make them feel HEY! This message may be relevant to me

One of the most powerful ways to learn is by discovering what NOT to do. Here's an example of how to write good

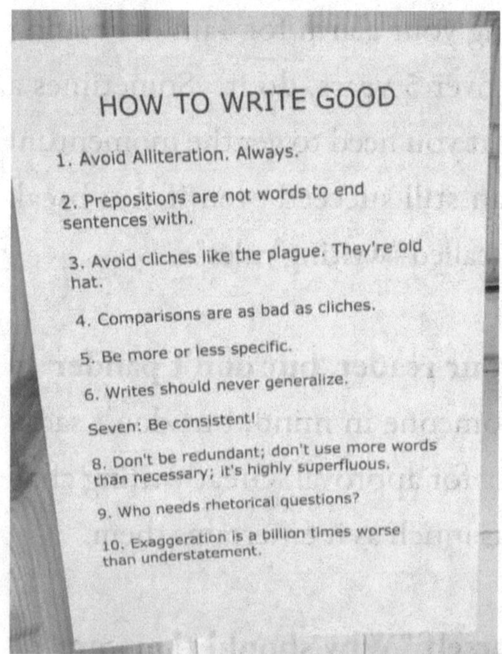

Chapter Twelve

Writing Style Comparisons

To draw a fair comparison of writing styles, I've taken a modest paragraph from **'Where My Heart Used To Be' by Sebastian Faulks** and held it up to the light of other authors, redressing it in their distinctive literary wardrobes to show how diversely the same small moment can be stitched, hemmed, and transfigured. Although some sentences appear to start and end in similar ways, the author's individuality filters through.

"I'll never see you again and I ought to try to give you some advice for the future. But the truth is I don't understand anything anymore. This is not the world I thought it was going to be. You'll have to make your own way in the mess we leave. Be kind

to other people, Be good to your mother." **Sebastian Faulks**

"I shall never see you again, and I suppose I ought to offer you some counsel for the years ahead. Yet honesty compels me to admit that I no longer understand very much at all. This is not the world I once imagined it would be. You must therefore make your own path through the confusion we leave behind us. Be kind to others, it matters more than you think. And above all, be good to your mother." **Ernest Hemingway**

"I shall never see you again, and I feel I ought to offer you some advice for what lies ahead. Yet the truth of it is that I no longer understand the world as I once did. It has turned out to be quite different from what I expected. You will have to find your own way through the disorder we leave behind. Try to be kind to other people. It is more important than it appears. And do be good to your mother." **Agatha Christie**

"I shall not see you again, and it seems only right that I should attempt to offer you some counsel for the future. Yet I must confess, with complete honesty, that I no longer understand the world as I once believed I did. It has not become what I expected. You will therefore have to forge your own path through the confusion we leave behind. Be kind to other people; it is a principle that endures even when much else fails. And be good to your mother." **Arthur Conan Doyle**

"II'll never see you again, and I suppose I should try to leave you with some advice for what comes next. The trouble is, I don't understand the world anymore. It isn't the one I thought I was preparing you for. You'll have to find your own path through the confusion we've made of it, and trust your own sense of right and wrong. Be kind to other people, even when it's difficult. And always, always be good to your mother." **J K Rowling**

"I shall never see you again, and I feel I ought to offer some advice for the future. Yet the honest

fact is that I no longer understand the world. It has not become what I believed it would be. You will have to make your own way through the confusion and damage we have left behind. Try to be kind to other people; it is a small decency, but not an unimportant one. And be good to your mother." **George Orwell**

"I will never see you again, and I feel I should leave you with some words for the road ahead. Yet the truth is that I no longer understand the world as I once did. It is not the world I imagined it would become. You will have to discover your own path through the chaos we have left behind, listening carefully to what your heart tells you. Be kind to other people, for kindness is never wasted. And always be good to your mother – she is part of your beginning and will always know the way back to yourself." **Paolo Coelho.**

"I shall behold thee nevermore, and yet I feel compelled to leave thee some small counsel for the days to come. But truth, plain and unadorned, must be

spoken: I understand the world no longer. This is not the shape I thought it would assume. Thou must therefore carve thy own passage through the ruin we have left behind. Be gentle with others, for such mercy is never lost. And above all else, be good to thy mother." **William Shakespeare**

Chapter Thirteen

Book Recommendations

I could fill pages on book recommendations, but I've always believed that preferences are personal. If I like a film, your opinion might differ. If I like music by an artist, you might not. If I like a book, you may have an altogether different view.

So I'm going to limit my recommendations to these:

"The Tall Lady With the Iceberg" **by** Anne Miller A truly valuable masterclass in metaphorical thinking.

"West With The Night" by Beryl Markham, is a luminous memoir by the first aviator to fly solo across the Atlantic against the wind, from east to west. In vivid, lyrical prose, she recalls a life shaped by the wild sweep of East Africa, its landscapes, dangers, and freedoms. The book is widely admired for its beauty and adventure, and even Ernest Hemingway conceded that Markham's writing surpassed that of many celebrated authors. Ernest Hemingway wrote "She can write rings around all of us who consider ourselves w riters... I wish you would get it and read it because it is really a bloody wonderful book".

"News From Tartary" By Peter Fleming (elder brother to James Bond author Ian Fleming) Beautifully written and masterly understated, this is not simply a superb account of a part of the world few of us will ever see, but also a marvellous insight into the last days of the Great Game, when Britain and Russia still faced each other across a Central Asia in a state of anarchy. It is a magnificent travelogue by one of the last and greatest adventures of Empire.

Graeme Dinnen

Other books by Graeme Dinnen:

Gum Disease: The Silent Battle In Your Mouth. Graeme Dinnen & Dr Elmar Jung. **htt ps://mybook.to/BattlingGumDisease**

Spice Trails: In The Footsteps of Nutmeg and Cloves. Graeme Dinnen. **https://mybook .to/SpiceTrails**

The Tao Of Putting: The Dance of Balance. Graeme Dinnen **https://mybook.to/TaoOfPutting**

Life In A Body: The Awakening. Phylipa Dinnen & Graeme Dinnen. **https://mybook.t o/LifeInABody**

Hitmaker's Handbook: How To Write Pop Songs That Stick. Graeme Dinnen. **https://m ybook.to/SongHandbook**

If **"Paint With Words"** offered you a moment, an idea, or a smile, do consider returning to Amazon where you bought "Paint With Words" and leave a short review. It might steer another curious reader toward something they'll truly value.